GOVERNOR

By Jacqueline Laks Gorman
Reading consultant: Susan Nations, M.Ed.,
author/literacy coach/consultant in literacy development

WEEKLY READER®
PUBLISHING

Please visit our web site at www.garethstevens.com
For a free color catalog describing our list of high-quality books,
call 1-800-542-2595 (USA) or 1-800-387-3178 (Canada). Our fax: 1-877-542-2596

Library of Congress Cataloging-in-Publication Data
Gorman, Jacqueline Laks, 1955–
    Governor / by Jacqueline Laks Gorman. — Updated ed.
      p. cm. — (Know your government)
    Includes bibliographical references and index.
    ISBN-10: 1-4339-0091-2 ISBN-13: 978-1-4339-0091-4 (lib. bdg.)
    ISBN-10: 1-4339-0119-6 ISBN-13: 978-1-4339-0119-5 (softcover)
    1. Governors—United States—Juvenile literature. I. Title.
  JK2447.G66   2008
  352.23'2130973—dc22   2008037310

This edition first published in 2009 by
Weekly Reader® Books
An Imprint of Gareth Stevens Publishing
1 Reader's Digest Road
Pleasantville, NY 10570-7000 USA

Executive Managing Editor: Lisa M. Herrington
Editors: Brian Fitzgerald and Barbara Kiely Miller
Creative Director: Lisa Donovan
Senior Designer: Keith Plechaty
Photo Researchers: Charlene Pinckney and Diane Laska-Swanke
Publisher: Keith Garton

Photo credits: cover & title page: © Mike Segar/Reuters/Corbis; p. 5 Chris Miller/AP; p. 6 Courtesy office of Gov. Bill Richardson; p. 7 North Wind Picture Archives; p. 9 Courtesy office of Gov. Janet Napolitano; p. 10 Courtesy office of Gov. Jodi Rell; p. 11 M. Spencer Green/AP; p. 12 Muscatine Journal, Beth Van Zandt/AP; p. 13 Jon C. Hancock/AP; p. 15 Chris Ochsner/ Topeka Capital-Journal/AP; p. 16 Bill Haber/AP; p. 17 Andy King/AP; p. 19 J. Scott Applewhite/AP; p. 20 Courtesy office of Gov. Deval Patrick; p. 21 Jim Wilson/AP/Pool.

Printed in the United States of America

1 2 3 4 5 6 7 8 9 10 09 08

Cover Photo: Arnold Schwarzenegger was elected governor of California in 2003. Before that, he was a famous movie star.

TABLE OF CONTENTS

Words that appear in the glossary are printed in **boldface** type the first time they appear in the text.

CHAPTER 1

Who Are Governors?

The president is the leader of the U.S. government. Each of the 50 states has its own government, too. Each state has its own **governor**. The governor is like the president of the state. He or she is in charge of the state government.

The U.S. government has three main branches, or parts. State governments are also split into three branches. The governor and his or her helpers form one branch. The other two branches of government pass the laws and rule on the laws.

Sarah Palin is the first female governor of Alaska. In 2008, she ran for vice president of the United States.

In May 2008, Governor Bill Richardson (right) of New Mexico met with the president of Mexico.

The governor is the leader of the state. He or she meets with the president and other leaders on behalf of the state. The governor also visits other countries for his or her state. Each governor has power only in his or her state, however.

The governor works in the capital city. For example, the governor of Maine works in Augusta, that state's capital city. The governor has an office in the state capitol building. Most governors live in their capital cities, too.

Augusta is the capital city of Maine. The state government offices have been in Maine's capitol building since 1832.

CHAPTER 2

What Does a Governor Do?

State governments have many jobs. They keep law and order. They watch over business. They take care of the environment. They also help run schools. Governors make sure that the state government runs smoothly.

The voters of a state **elect**, or choose, many people in the state government. The governor picks many others who work for the state. He or she may also pick some of the top judges in the state.

In March 2008, Governor Janet Napolitano of Arizona read to students in her state.

In 2008, Connecticut Governor Jodi Rell (seated) signed a bill into law. The new law helps protect wildlife in her state.

Each state has a **legislature**. The people in the legislature pass new state laws. Ideas for new laws are called **bills**. The legislature sends bills to the governor. He or she must sign a bill before it becomes a law. The governor then makes sure that people in the state follow the law.

The governor and the legislature also decide how to spend the state's money. They work together on the state **budget**. The budget is a plan for spending and raising money. The budget includes money to pay for schools, hospitals, and new roads.

A state's budget includes money to build and fix highways.

In June 2008, Governor Chet Culver of Iowa helped fill sandbags in a city where there was a flood.

The governor works with the legislature to fix problems in the state. The governor also helps people in the state during an emergency. Some governors also head the troops and state police who protect the people in the state.

Many states have the same problems. Governors sometimes meet to try to solve these problems. Governors also travel on business for their state. They may visit other states. They may try to get other countries to buy products made in their state.

All the governors in the United States meet at least once a year. They talk about ways to fix problems in their states.

CHAPTER 3

How Does a Person Become Governor?

All governors are elected by voters in the state. The rules for becoming governor are not the same in every state, however. In many states, the governor must be at least 30 years old. He or she must have lived in the state for a certain number of years.

In most states, voters pick the governor every four years. The people in New Hampshire and Vermont vote for governor every two years.

In some states, a person can be governor as many times as the voters want. In other states, a governor can serve only two **terms** in office.

Governor Kathleen Sebelius of Kansas was re-elected in 2006. Her state allows the governor to serve only two terms.

People who run for office are called **candidates**. Most candidates for governor are from one of the two main **political parties**: the Democratic Party and the Republican Party. Candidates for governor share their ideas with voters in many ways.

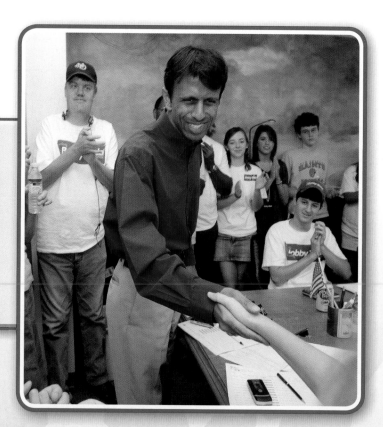

Republican Bobby Jindal ran for governor of Louisiana in 2007. He became the first Indian American governor in history.

Tim Pawlenty was re-elected governor of Minnesota in 2006. He thanked voters after his win.

Candidates travel all over the state. They talk to voters and give speeches. People across the state vote on Election Day. The candidate with the most votes is elected governor.

CHAPTER 4

Famous Governors

The United States has had many famous governors. Some did great things for their state. Others helped the whole nation. Some governors even went on to become president of the United States.

George W. Bush (left) and Bill Clinton (right) were governors before they became president.

Thomas Jefferson was the first former governor to become president. He was governor of Virginia from 1779 to 1781. He later became the third president of the United States.

Some recent U.S. presidents were former governors. Bill Clinton was governor of Arkansas. George W. Bush was governor of Texas.

In 1990, Douglas Wilder of Virginia made history. He became the first African American to be elected governor. In 2007, Deval Patrick became the second African American to be elected governor. He was elected governor of Massachusetts.

In June 2008, Governor Deval Patrick visited children at a hospital in Massachusetts.

In 2007, wildfires destroyed homes in California. Governor Arnold Schwarzenegger helped people stay strong during that tough time.

For years, people knew Arnold Schwarzenegger as a movie star. In 2003, he was elected governor of California. He was re-elected in 2006. He gives all of his pay as governor to charity. Like all governors, he works hard to help the people in his state.

Glossary

bills: written plans for new laws

budget: a plan for how to spend and make money

candidates: people who are running for office

elect: to choose leaders by voting

governor: the head of a state government

legislature: the part of the government that makes the laws

political parties: groups of people who have similar beliefs and ideas

terms: set periods of time that a person serves in office

To Find Out More

Books

State Government. Kaleidoscope: Government (series).
Suzanne Levert (Benchmark Books, 2003)

What's a Governor? First Guide to Government (series).
Nancy Harris (Heinemann, 2007)

Web Sites

A Day in the Life of a Governor
www.state.nj.us/governor/kids
Find out what the governor of New Jersey does during a typical day.

Kids.gov—State Web Sites
www.kids.gov/k_5/k_5_states.shtml
This site includes links to many sites that have information about states and their governors.

Publisher's note to educators and parents: Our editors have carefully reviewed these web sites to ensure that they are suitable for children. Many web sites change frequently, however, and we cannot guarantee that a site's future contents will continue to meet our high standards of quality and educational value. Be advised that children should be closely supervised whenever they access the Internet.

Index

About the Author

Jacqueline Laks Gorman is a writer and an editor. She grew up in New York City. She has worked on many kinds of books and has written several children's series. She lives with her husband, David, and children, Colin and Caitlin, in DeKalb, Illinois. She registered to vote when she turned 18 and votes in every election.